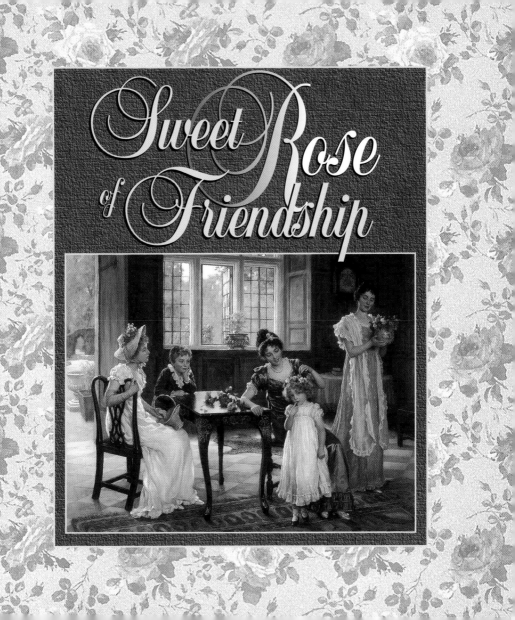

# Sweet Rose of Friendship

# Illustration Credits

Copyright © 1995
Brownlow Publishing Company
6309 Airport Freeway
Fort Worth, Texas 76117

ISBN 1-57051-043-1

*Cover/Interior:*
Koechel Peterson & Associates

Printed in USA

# Sweet Rose of Friendship

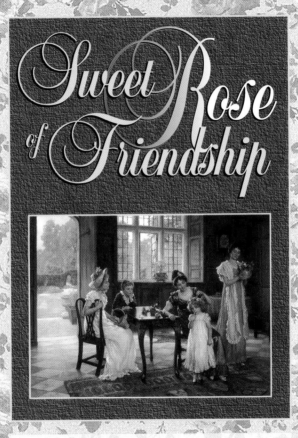

*Edited by* Paul C. Brownlow

*Brownlow*

Brownlow Publishing Company, Inc.

*So shall a friendship*

*fill each heart*

*With perfume*

*sweet as roses are,*

*That even though*

*we be apart,*

*We'll scent the*

*fragrance from afar.*

GEORGIA MCCOY

*I am*

*the rose of Sharon,*

*and the lily*

*of the valleys.*

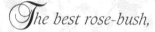

SONG OF SOLOMON 2:1

*The best rose-bush,*

*after all,*

*is not that which*

*has the fewest thorns*

*but that which bears*

*the finest roses.*

HENRY VAN DYKE

*The only rose*

*without thorns*

*is friendship.*

DE SCUDERI

*He that*

*plants thorns*

*must never expect*

*to gather roses.*

PILPAY

# There's Nothing
# Like the Rose

The lily has an air,

And the snowdrop a grace,

And the sweet-pea a way,

And the heart's-ease a face,—

Yet there's nothing like the rose

When she blows.

CHRISTINA G. ROSSETTI

# Rose Petal Sorbet

¾ cup sugar

2 cups water

Juice and pared rind of 2 lemons

1½ cups scented rose petals

2 teaspoons triple-distilled rose water

1 egg white

In a pan, dissolve the sugar in the water. Add lemon rind. Bring to boil, then simmer for 6 minutes. Remove from heat, add the rose petals, then leave to cool. Strain syrup, add lemon juice. Flavor with rose water. Freeze in covered plastic container until mushy, then whisk in stiffly beaten egg white. Freeze until firm. Allow to soften slightly before serving in chilled glasses. ❧

# The Rose

There is probably no inanimate object in the world more beautiful than a delicately tinted Rose. There is certainly nothing else which combines such beauty of form and color with such exquisite delicacy of texture and such delicious perfume. The charm seems to me to lie, in great part, in the fine silky texture of the petals and in their translucency. It is the charm which it shares with every beautiful thing which is "hidden yet half revealed."

GEORGE C. LAMBDIN

# The Roses of Today

One of the most tragic things I know about human nature is that all of us tend to put off living. We are all dreaming of some magical rose garden over the horizon—instead of enjoying the roses that are blooming outside our windows today.

DALE CARNEGIE

There should be beds of Roses, banks of Roses, bowers of Roses, hedges of Roses, edgings of Roses, pillars of Roses, arches of Roses, fountains of Roses, baskets of Roses, vistas and alleys of the Rose.

DEAN HOLE

*Make hearts happy,*

*roses grow,*

*Let the friends*

*around you know*

*The love you have*

*before they go;*

*Show it now.*

ANONYMOUS

# Old Friends

There are no friends like old friends,
And none so good and true;
We greet them when we meet them,
As roses greet the dew;
No other friends are dearer,
Though born of kindred mold;
And while we prize the new ones,
We treasure more the old.

There are no friends like old friends,
Where'er we dwell or roam,
In lands beyond the ocean,
Or near the bounds of home;
And when they smile to gladden,
Or sometimes frown to guide,
We fondly wish those old friends
Were always by our side.

*There are no friends like old friends,*
*To calm our frequent fears,*
*When shadows fall and deepen*
*Through life's declining years;*
*And when our faltering footsteps*
*Approach the Great Divide,*
*We'll long to meet the old friends*
*Who wait the other side.*

DAVID BANKS SICKLES

How fair is the Rose!

What a beautiful flower.

The glory of April and May!

But the leaves are beginning

to fade in an hour,

And they wither and die in a day.

Yet the Rose has

one powerful virtue to boast,

Above all the flowers of the field;

When its leaves are all dead,

and fine colors are lost,

Still how sweet a perfume it will yield!

ISAAC WATTS

O Rose, thou flower of flowers, thou fragrant wonder,
Who shall describe thee in thy ruddy prime;
Thy perfect fulness in the summer time;
When the pale leaves blushingly part asunder
And show the warm red heart lies glowing under?
Thou shouldst bloom surely in some sunny clime,
Untouched by blights and chilly Winter's rime,
Where lightnings never flash, nor peals the thunder.
And yet in happier spheres they cannot need thee
So much as we do with our weight of woe;
Perhaps they would not tend, perhaps not need thee,
And thou wouldst lonely and neglected grow;
And He Who is All-Wise, He hath decreed thee
To gladden earth and cheer all hearts below.

CHRISTINA G. ROSSETTI

# A Rose Is a Rose

## A Short History of Roses

Fossilized rose leaves found in some parts of the world suggest that roses may have grown several million years ago, but the first written mention of the rose comes from Sumerian tablets dated about 3000 B.C. About 1800 B.C., roses were cultivated in the royal gardens of Knossos, Crete, and were depicted with other flowers in the palace frescoes.

Ancient gardens throughout the known world produced roses in abundance. In Persia, for example, roses became so popular that the Persian word for rose and flower was the same. The Chinese also became quite fond of roses and cultivated them in Peking as early as 500 B.C. The Greeks used the rose extensively in their mythological tales, depicting Aphrodite and her followers as clothed in wreaths of white roses and walking on rose-strewn paths.

But of all the early cultural groups, the Romans were the most lavish and extravagant in their love for and use of roses. Rose wreaths were awarded for great military achievements. Nero showered rose petals from the ceiling on his dinner guests, who stood on a rose-petal carpet. Lovers exchanged rose wreaths. Roses were eaten, and rose wines were savored with meals. The poet Horace finally wrote that too many roses were grown in Rome and not enough corn.

And because of the rose's close association with pagan Rome, it fell out of favor during the rise of Christianity. In fact, roses nearly vanished in Europe. During this time, most of the roses were grown in monasteries by monks who used them mainly for medicinal purposes.

In the twelfth and thirteenth centuries, however, the returning Crusaders brought roses back to Europe with them. They also brought back Greek and Latin texts that revealed a great knowledge of cultivating the species of roses that had disappeared from Europe. As the harsh aceticism of the medieval period gradually waned, the rose began to regain its popularity in all phases of life.

# From Friendship's Hand

Only a little rose, you see,

From friendship's hand I come to thee.

She plucked and said, "Go, rosebud, go,"

And then she whispered o'er me low,

"Oh, would his heart were pure tonight

As thou, dear rosebud, fresh and bright."

She whispered low, "Go, rosebud sweet,

And tell him, tho' we ne'er may meet,

An earnest prayer I'll for him send,

That God may keep him to the end."

Only a little rose, you see,

From friendship's hand I come to thee.

GEORGIA McCOY

*In the garden*

*suspended in time,*

*my mother sits*

*in a redwood chair;*

*light fills the sky,*

*the folds of her dress,*

*the roses tangled*

*beside her.*

MARK STRAND

# The Language of the Rose

Rose ❧ Love

Austrian Rose ❧ Thou art all that is lovely

Boule de Neige Rose ❧ Only for thee

Bridal Rose ❧ Happy love

Burgundy Rose ❧ Unconscious beauty

Cabbage Rose ❧ Ambassador of love

Campion Rose ❧ Only deserve my love

Carolina Rose ❧ Love is dangerous

Charles le Fievree Rose ❧ Speak low if you speak love

China Rose ❧ Beauty always new

Christmas Rose ❧ Relieve my anxiety

Daily Rose ❧ Thy smile I aspire to

Damask Rose ❧ Brilliant complexion

Deep Red Rose ❧ Bashful shame

Dog Rose ❧ Pleasure and pain

*Gloire de Dijon Rose* ❧ *A messenger of love*
*Guelder Rose* ❧ *Winter, age*
*Hundred-Leaved Rose* ❧ *Pride*
*Japan Rose* ❧ *Beauty is your only attraction*
*John Hopper Rose* ❧ *Encouragement*
*La France Rose* ❧ *Meet me by moonlight*
*Maiden Blush Rose* ❧ *If you love me you will find it out*
*Monteflora Rose* ❧ *Grace*
*Mundi Rose* ❧ *Variety*
*Musk Rose* ❧ *Capricious beauty*
*Nephitos Rose* ❧ *Infatuation*
*Single Rose* ❧ *Simplicity*
*Thornless Rose* ❧ *Early attachment*
*Unique Rose* ❧ *Call me not beautiful*
*White Rose* ❧ *I am worthy of you*
*White and Red Roses* ❧ *Unity*
*Yellow Rose* ❧ *Decrease of love, jealousy*

THE LANGUAGE OF FLOWERS

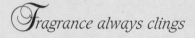

*Fragrance always clings
to the hand that
gives you roses.*

*Some people complain
because God put thorns on roses,
while others praise Him
for putting roses among thorns.*

*Where you tend a rose,
my lad, a thistle cannot grow.*

## Roses

You love the roses—so do I. I wish

The sky would rain down roses, as they rain

From off the shaken bush. Why will it not?

Then all the valley would be pink and white

And soft to tread on. They would fall as light

As feathers, smelling sweet: and it would be

Like sleeping and yet waking, all at once.

GEORGE ELIOT

# No Friend Like an Old Friend

There is no friend like the old friend
who has shared our morning days,
No greeting like his welcome,
no homage like his praise;
Fame is the scentless sunflower,
with gaudy crown of gold;
But friendship is the breathing rose,
with sweets in every fold.

OLIVER WENDELL HOLMES

# Candied Rose Petals

1 egg white
sugar
fresh rose petals and leaves

Gently beat egg white in a small bowl. Sprinkle sugar on a plate. Dip rose petals and leaves in egg white, then in sugar. Dry on rack, then layer on wax paper with paper towel between each layer.

Display candied rose petals on candy tray, as cake decoration or garnish for fruit cup. ❧

# Sweeter Than Honey

O sweeter than the honey well,
Deep in the sweetest rose of June,
And all sweet things the tongue can tell
On clover-scented afternoon,
Is friendship that has lived for years
Through fortune, failure, and through tears.

Though he who wears it sacredly
Be swarted like the rafters are
That shelter him, eternity
May hold few jewels half so rare!
And God will find for such a friend
Some sweeter slumber in the end.

ALLAN BOTSFORD

# Pleasant Roses

May pleasant
Roses without thorns
Bloom in beauty at your feet,
May your life be sweet,
Like a song in tune,
And with time unfold,
Like a rose in June!
Like a tune which flows
All the bright day long
With no bar of grief
In its happy song!
Like a rose from which
All the bright day through
Hours like busy bees,
Gather sweets for you!

K. S. COWAN

*Beautiful Rose in fragrance so rare,*
*Painted in colors bright,*
*Born of the sun and pure gladsome air,*
*Fed by the dews of night.*

J. H. KURZENKNABE

'Tis the last rose of summer
Left blooming alone;
All her lovely companions
Are faded and gone;
No flower of her kindred,
No rose-bud is nigh,
To reflect back her blushes,
Or give sigh for sigh.

THOMAS MOORE

Red Rose, proud Rose,
sad Rose of all my days!
Come near me,
while I sing the ancient ways.

WILLIAM BUTLER YEATS

Two roses on one slender spray
In sweet communion grew,
Together hailed the morning ray
And drank the evening dew.

MONTGOMERY

# Friendship Fair

Through thee alone the sky is arched,
Through thee the rose is red;
All things through thee take nobler form,
And look beyond the earth,
The mill-round of our fate appears
A sun-path in thy worth.
Me too thy nobleness has taught
To master my despair;
The fountains of my hidden life
Are through thy friendship fair.

RALPH WALDO EMERSON

*A rose too often smelled
loses its fragrance.*

SPANISH PROVERB

*Each rose that comes brings me greetings
from the Rose of an eternal spring.*

RABINDRANATH TAGORE

*God gave us memories that we might
have roses in December.*

JAMES M. BARRIE

*Sweet as fragrant roses
'Tis to have a friend
On whom in gloom or sunshine
We know we can depend.*

NINETEENTH-CENTURY
CALLING CARD

# The Empress of Roses

While the rose was slowly gaining in popularity among the English between the years 1400 and 1800, Empress Josephine of France, first wife of Napoleon I, promoted the rose's return to prominence in Europe and the "rose renaissance."

Josephine's love for roses began in her childhood on the island of Martinique. When Napoleon presented her with the country estate Malmaison in 1798, she determined to grow every known variety and to make Malmaison the most famous rose garden of its time. She preferred the English roses and the naturalistic English landscape style, and hired André Dupont from the Luxembourg Palace to assemble and cultivate her collection.

Even war did not stop Josephine's march to rose excellence. Napoleon's armies were instructed to collect and send roses back to Malmaison from anywhere. In spite of the hostilities between England and France, Josephine commissioned an English nurseryman to travel freely between the two countries to promote the growth of roses at Malmaison. The British naval fleet cooperated fully and allowed him and all ships carrying seeds and plants to proceed safely.

Josephine spent enormous sums of money on her gardens and at her death in 1814 left enormous debts. The gardens were neglected until 1904, when they were restored on a much smaller scale and presented to the French government.

*K*indness is
like a rose,
which though
easily crushed
and fragile,
yet speaks
a language of
silent power.

FRANCES J. ROBERTS

*A*ll the world
glows with
roses, roses, roses.

SAUL CHERNIHOVSKY

# Love Planted a Rose

Love planted a rose,

And the world turned sweet,

Where the wheatfield blows,

Love planted a rose.

Up the mill-wheel's prose

Ran a music beat.

Love planted a rose,

And the world turned sweet.

KATHARINE LEE BATES

# The English Rose Garden

An English garden without Roses would be an incomplete and soulless thing. I do not say that every garden should include in its design a Rose garden. There are, however, many advantages in allotting some portion of the grounds mainly to the culture of Roses, and it is almost inevitable that sooner or later some part of the garden becomes known as such. Not the least advantage of this giving over one portion of the garden to Roses is the fact that the results obtained thereby are, generally speaking, far more satisfactory than by attempting to grow them mixed up with other things. The Rose is one of those plants that thrives best in a state of splendid isolation. It objects to being associated with anything else. It needs a sort of special treatment that is not applicable to many other garden flowers.

It will, however, be universally conceded that the Rose is worth this exalted position in the garden. What else is there that gives us such variety of form and colour, such an extended period of blooming, such adaptable habits of growth that there can be found, sorts that will climb over a house and cover the roof with flower, or provide a neat and glowing edging to a border, and achieve almost everything the garden requires in between these two extremes? It is because they are sufficient in themselves for most garden purposes that they have appropriated a place in the English garden that is held by no other flower.

GEORGE DILLISTONE

*What's in a name?*

*That which we call a rose*

*By any other name*

*would smell as sweet.*

Wᴵʟʟᴵᴀᴍ Sʜᴀᴋᴇsᴘᴇᴀʀᴇ

*The wilderness*

*and the solitary place*

*shall be glad for them;*

*and the desert shall rejoice,*

*and blossom as the rose.*

Isᴀᴵᴀʜ 35:1

# Rose Petal Tea

*2 tablespoons strongly scented,*
*dried rose petals*
*3 ½ cups large leaf China tea*

Mix together and store in airtight tin.
Prepare tea as usual but serve without milk
or lemon.

# Rose Garden Cake

*sponge cake*
*fresh strawberries*
*rose petal jam*
*whipped cream*
*toasted almonds or coconut*

Cut out center of sponge cake and fill with strawberries, rose petal jam and whipped cream. Cover whole cake with whipped cream. Sprinkle with almonds or coconut. Decorate with a few pink rose blooms.

*He who would have
beautiful Roses in his garden
must have beautiful Roses
in his heart.*

Dean Hole

*God of the Granite and the Rose!*

*Soul of the Sparrow and the Bee!*

*The mighty tide of Being flows*

*Through countless channels, Lord, from Thee.*

Lizzie Doten

# My Mother's Rose Garden

The gardens of my youth were fragrant gardens and it is their sweetness rather than their patterns or their furnishings that I now most clearly recall. My mother's rose garden in Maryland was famous in that countryside and in the nearby city, for many shared its bounty. In it grew the most fragrant roses, not only great bushes of Provence, Damask and Gallica roses, but a collection of the finest teas and Noisettes of the day. Maréchal Niel, Lamarque and Gloire de Dijon climbed high on trellises against the stone of the old house and looked in at the second-story windows. I remember that some sort of much coveted distinction was conferred upon the child finding the first long golden bud of Maréchal Niel.

LOUISE BEEBE WILDER

*What other planet smells of roses?*
PAM BROWN